I0490026

Recession Reality Check

By Ade Asefeso MCIPS MBA

Second Edition

ISBN-13: 978-1499702231

ISBN-10: 149970223X

Publisher: AA Global Sourcing Ltd
Website: http://www.aaglobalsourcing.com

Table of Contents

Disclaimer

This publication is designed to provide competent and reliable information regarding the subject matter covered. However, it is sold with the understanding that the author and publisher are not engaged in rendering professional advice. The authors and publishers specifically disclaim any liability that is incurred from the use or application of contents of this book.

If you purchased this book without a cover you should be aware that this book may have been stolen property and reported as "unsold and destroyed" to the publisher. In this case neither the author nor the publisher has received any payment for this "stripped book."

Dedication

To my family and friends who seems to have been sent here to teach me something about who I am supposed to be. They have nurtured me, challenged me, and even opposed me…. But at every juncture has taught me!

This book is dedicated to my lovely boys, Thomas, Michael and Karl. Teaching them to manage their finance will give them the lives they deserve. They have taught me more about life, presence, and energy management than anything I have done in my life.

Chapter 1: What is a Recession?

This happens when there is a significant decline in the economy which usually lasts for a short period of time. You can tell there is one when consumers don't spend that much, a lot of people are unemployed, companies have to make job cuts, industrial production is down and lately, there is a housing crisis as people have to foreclose their homes.

The technical indicator which tells you that the country is in a recession is when there has been 2 consecutive quarters of negative growth which is measured by the country's GDP or gross domestic product.

Experts say that this is bound to happen because it is part of the business cycle and things usually improve within 16 to 18 months.

What is a business cycle? It is considered to be a periodic but irregular up and down movement in a country's economic activity which can be measured by fluctuations in the GDP as well as other macroeconomic variables.

Things are going up when the economy recovers and expands. The situation goes the opposite direction when the market experiences a slowdown until it eventually reaches a recession.

But there has never been such a drastic move when the country was in recession. In the past, lowering interest rates was the solution. In 2007, the Federal government slashed the interest rate three times towards the end of the third and fourth quarter so that banks could get overnight loans for as low as 4.25%.

The recession in the United States has affected other countries and drastic steps have been taken to prevent it from getting worse. Britain unveiled plans to inject up to 50 billion pounds which is equivalent to $90 billion into its biggest retail banks. Members of the European Union agree that there must be reforms in the world's financial system.

Is there light at the end of the tunnel? The answer is yes but it is going to be some time before anyone will see any improvements. In fact, this crisis could continue on to whoever wins the Presidential election next time making it one of the key issues.

During the last three Presidential debates, both candidates were asked what they are going to do to fight the current recession. One of them insisted on tax cuts while the other believes that another approach has to be used.

As we all know Obama won. Since then he has been working on plan to get the unemployed back to work so that the current state of the economy could improve. It is something that the American public are looking at during Obama term as president and when the dust settles, only then will people be able to say whether or not this person was the right one for the job or they should have voted for the other candidate so we can get out of this recession.

Did you know that economic recession is actually ordered in the Bible? Every 49 years the people of Israel were ordered to celebrate a year of Jubilee, where the land would lie fallow and all property would be returned to its original owner. This year and the following year there would be no new crops, so the people were required to prepare. Imagine: Every 50 years they Israelites knew there was going to be an economic recession.

If you could predict when an economic recession would occur, what would you do? Would you just step back and allow it to happen, or do you think that you would take steps to prepare yourself and your company to weather the storm? Do you think you might even study the trends and find a way to make that economic recession work for you? Maybe store away a little bit extra during those forty nine years so that you could see to the people who didn't have the foresight to put away what they needed to get by those two years of famine?

That is what we are going to be discussing in the next couple of sections. What you need to do to help yourself ride out a recession without losing everything you've worked so hard for, and what you can do to make this recession work for you. Remember, recession is nothing new. Men and women have been surviving recessions for as long as there has been an economy to recede.

Chapter 2: We are in a Recession

There is no doubt that we are in a recession. What you have to answer for yourself now is what are you going to do about it? On your own, you can't change it but you can adapt to the situation until things blow over.

Now how do we do that? Well the best thing to do is tighten your belt because the credit market is frozen so you won't be able to get a loan for personal or for business purposes.

With the money you have, it is best to use it wisely by buying only the important items when you go to the grocery stores. If there are other items you want to go get, you have to sacrifice in order to get it by buying different brand that is more affordable. Since most supermarkets have special offers, give out free vouchers or samples, you should also avail of it.

Do you drive yourself to work? If you do, has it ever occurred to you how much you spend on gas everyday? If you drive an SUV, chances are you spend a lot on gas just to go to and from work. Part of tightening that belt means trading in your SUV for a smaller car. If it is possible, go for a hybrid because you save on gas and get a tax break from the government.

Most people eat out during their lunch break. Instead of buying food, why don't they prepare it at home and then bring it to the office. That way, you don't have to spend your hard earned dollars for lunch so you can use this elsewhere.

Your employer is aware of the current financial crisis. You can help him or her by suggesting if it will be possible to do some of the work at home. Some companies allow their employees to do this so just have to check if this scenario can work for you. Just be sure that you are as productive at home like you are in the office.

But because you spend more time at home instead of the office, your electricity bill will surely go up. To try and resolve that, the best thing to do will be to replace your lighting fixtures with those that consume less wattage. Since you have a landline and mobile phone, you should change this with a provider that offers better rates than what you are currently paying for. The same goes for other bills that pay monthly.

With all the money you are able to save, you should use it to pay any outstanding debts that you may have with the bank to ensure you have a good credit rating. You can also use this to take up a training course or go back to school to be able to shift to another career if the current one you are in right now is not working out.

The current recession isn't going to end by Christmas since it is forecasted to last until next year in some counties. For you to survive, you have to tighten your belt. If you don't know how to do this or want to learn more, it is best to hire a financial adviser who can come up with a plan so you can just follow it.

Chapter 3: A Recession is a Fact of Life

Believe it or not, a recession is a fact of life. Why? Because it is part of the business cycle and this is bound to happen when the economy expands, slows down until it hits rocks bottom and then recover once again.

The only difference between a recession and this recession we are experience is that this problem does not happen often. It may take years before this happens again and in the world history, the last time we had a recession in US and Europe was 2000.

When it does happen, experts won't admit that it is there even if everyone around knows that it is. How? By looking at various factors which include consumer spending, the unemployment rate, industrial production, real income and wholesale trade.

One solution to help stimulate the economy is to lower the interest rate. But since this is not enough to make the problem go away, we have to do our share until this is over. Companies have to make job cuts but the bad news is that you put more people out of work because this is the only way to stay in business.

But is putting people out of work the only solution for a business to survive? Some experts disagree because if the company is able to focus on customer service, lower price points and make cuts elsewhere, you help prevent the unemployment rate from getting higher.

On your end, if you still have a job, you have to spend less because the prices of goods will go up which is why you only have to buy the essentials. One thing you have to cut down is your fuel expenses so you might want to trade in your SUV for a smaller car that has better gas mileage.

To make sure you are not on the list of the next people to be axed, find ways to make yourself valuable in the office by taking on other responsibilities. If this is not enough to put money on the table, see if you can get a second job until the situation improves.

There is an upside to a recession. If you need money, you can borrow at a lower interest rate and you will be able to buy stocks, bonds and property at very affordable prices.

A recession is a fact of life and if you think that this happens only in the US, it has happened in other countries as well. What makes this current one so different from others in the past is the fact that what started in the US is now spreading around the world which is why nations are talking to one another to help prevent it from getting worse.

How long will this recession last? It is anybody's guess but this will last until the end of the year with hopes that things will improve by the first or second quarter of next year. How it affects people will be different depending on their current financial situation so before it is too late, save up. If you can, invest in a few things which you know will make you money in the future. For those who are unsure, you better hire a financial planner so you are safe if ever life throws you a fastball.

Chapter 4: What to do during a Recession

Setting up an emergency fund will be very useful especially when there is a recession. This will enable you to survive several months without worrying if you still have money to buy stuff especially when there is a slowdown.

But when it hits you, cleaning up your balance sheet is just one way to survive the financial crisis. To help you along, here are a few other ideas which you may find useful.

In 2008, the unemployment rate grew by 6.1%, its highest level in 5 years. The last time it hit this mark was in 2003 as the economy was still recovering from the 2000-2001 recession. These job cuts happened in the airline, travel, retail and service industry just to name a few. If you happen to work in one of these industries, you should probably consider a career shift to an occupation that is more stable even if it means going back to school.

Going to school is not an option if you are raising a family. The next best thing to do will be take an extra job. Just make sure that the time you spend here does not affect your primary job otherwise, you could lose it.

Most Americans have invested in the stock market and if you are one of them don't panic and think about selling it just because things are down. You have to remember that a recession is cyclical so your portfolio will recover in the future. You just have to be patient because it is going to take several months before everything is back to normal.

But if you do have the money, now is the best time to buy stocks and bonds. Why? Because these are relatively cheap and you can cash it in when the economy is back on track.

Apart from going back to school and getting a second job, perhaps you can use your skills and then offer this as a service to others. If you like to cook, make some pastries and then sell these to potential stores. If you are good with your hands, maybe you can help repair leaks should your neighbour have a problem with their plumbing.

If you own an SUV, trade it in for a small vehicle because you get better mileage with a smaller car. If you have the money, see if you can get one that is a hybrid because apart from consuming less gas, you get tax breaks for investing in alternative forms of energy.

When you go to the grocery stores, only buy the essentials. Resist the urge to buy things that the kids want. If you can't say no, try to get a similar brand that is just as good as what they want.

Lastly, we all have bills to pay monthly. If possible, switch to better and more affordable services because each penny counts during these dire times.

There are other ways to survive a recession apart from those mentioned. By following these tips and getting advice from a financial planner, you are sure to wither out this storm. Until that day comes, you shouldn't live in fear but rather make the most of it because this isn't the first time that you will face a recession and it surely won't be the last.

Chapter 5: Keeping your Business Floating Until the Flood Waters are Gone

If you are the owner of a business you are going to have a much more personal view of the effects of the economic recession, because it is going to be your profit margin that is beginning to show a loss. It is times like these when many business owners find themselves wishing that they could go back to the days of being a mere employee, because then all they had to worry about was whether or not they were going to keep their job-not whether or not their investment was about to come crashing down around their heads and leave them in debt and bankrupt.

The good news is that if you are a business owner facing the inevitability of an economic recession you are in a unique position to take advantage of it. An economic recession can be the savvy business owner's best friend if you know how to use the opportunities that only present themselves in times of hardship like these. If you are prepared to take the steps you need to take in order to make those opportunities a reality; then you are in a perfect opportunity to ensure that when all those other businesses out there are floundering yours continues to thrive.

Chapter 6: How Low can you Go?

The first thing you have to remember is that an economic recession happens for a reason, and that reason is that people are trying to hold on to their money like they are afraid the next Great Depression is waiting right around the corner for them. You are not going to be able to pry that money out of your customers and clients with clever marketing strategies. They are far too clever for that (or so they would like you to think).

If you can't get money out of them the old fashioned way, how are you going to keep your business afloat? By doing what businessmen and women have been doing for centuries to make sure that they stay on the top of their game. You are going to undercut your competition!

Think of it this way. If you only had fifty dollars in your pocket and you needed to buy a new lamp for your home, where would you be more likely to go to purchase that lamp? To an expensive retailer that specializes in high quality lamps and might have something that was only a little scratched or chipped for fifty dollars or your local Wal-Mart, where you can purchase a perfectly fine lamp for half that amount that will be more than serviceable until you have the money to buy something high quality that will last?

If you are looking at this and wondering why anyone would pass up the opportunity to get a once in a lifetime deal on a decent lamp you obviously haven't looked at Wal-Mart's financial reports lately. There is a reason that Wal-Mart is one of the top retailers in the country, and it's not because it offers high quality, one of a kind items. It's because it offers mediocre, generic but necessary items cheap.

Stores like Wal-Mart thrive in times of economic recession like this because even those shoppers who turned their nose up at the idea of shopping someplace so completely lacking in designer brand labels will view things a little differently when their budget doesn't allow for them to continue living the lavish lifestyle to which they have grown accustomed. They are thrust into a position where they will dominate the retail market because they are able to offer a wide variety of the basic and not so basic necessities of daily living (like living room lamps) at a price dramatically lower than that of their competitors.

You want to take a page out of Wal-Mart's book. During an economic recession people are looking for ways they can save money, even if it means accepting slightly inferior quality products and services. If you can offer them top of the line products and services for a lower price than your competition, you will have done three things:

1) Ensured that you have a steady stream of profit coming in at a time when most businesses are losing money. If you can convince these customers that you deserve to have their business you will be able to keep money flowing steadily into your pocket-and you

better believe they are going to tell their money-conscious friends.

2) Stolen them away from your competition. Loyalty is a beautiful thing in the business world. As a general rule, when consumers find a provider or supplier that they are happy with they will continue to do business with them to continue enjoying that same smooth relationship even if it means they have to spend a little extra.

An economic recession takes loyalty like that and throws it out of the window, because when you get down to it most people are far more worried about the state of their own pocketbook than they are about whether or not a company they happen to do business with stays in business. If you can offer your goods and services at a lower price than your competition you can rest assured that you are going to be enjoying their business for a long time to come.

3) You have cemented your future. As I mentioned above, consumers develop an incredible sense of loyalty for the providers of their goods and services when the experience has been good. By stepping in and offering them a great deal you have laid the foundation for building a fantastic relationship with your customers, and while you continue to offer them that same great deal you are guaranteeing that even when the economy picks back up you will keep their business and their loyalty.

Regardless of how dirty or underhanded it may feel take the time to shop around and see what your competition is charging-then deliberately undercut them. Remember, all is fair in love and war, and when it comes to helping your business through an economic recession it is definitely a war.

Chapter 7: Keep your Business Macro

The number one thing that the shift to e-commerce has taught us is that with the huge amount of competition we face out on the market, if we want to have a chance at succeeding we need to specialize. Tackling a large niche is simply too risky, and you are going to be facing so much competition that your consumers are going to walk away long before they know what you have to offer in favour of someone who clearly is going to be able to give them what they want.

An economic recession is the exception to the rule. During an economic recession people's primary motivation is going to be to save as much money as humanly possible, and while that recession is gradually weeding its way through your competition you want to be able to step in and pick up as many of the pieces as possible.

What am I talking about? Let's say that your business specializes in providing transportation services between the Greyhound station and the local universities of a major city. Good work if you can get it! Then an economic recession hits, and people are beginning to find it more economical to either walk or hop public transportation as opposed to maintaining and parking a car or calling a taxi.

Suddenly you are faced with a dilemma. There are literally hundreds of people every day leaving the Greyhound station for parts unknown in the city, and every one of those people needs a ride because they refuse to waste their precious money on private transportation. They are not all college students, however, and they are not going to be dependably heading between one university or another.

What do you do? Do you simply allow this opportunity to pass you by, or do you expand your horizons a little?

This is an excellent example of how an economic recession can help a business by subsequently driving to it a client base that it might not otherwise have had. There is very little chance that any of these people would have been interested in hopping a ride to the local university unless they were headed someplace nearby, but if you were willing to spread your wings a little bit and provide transportation to various points throughout the city rather than simply the universities you could potentially open the door to quadrupling your profit margin.

Your business will grow because it will become more macro, less specialized and more generalized in a nod to the need of the people around you. This is in direct opposition to what you have been told regarding the development of businesses in today's economy, but guess what?

A changing economy = A changing business

If your business is going to survive this recession without lifelong consequences it can only do so if it is willing to change and adapt. Do you remember when we mentioned earlier about the need to become more diverse and put your fingers in more pies in your company in order to recession proof your job? Just because the quantity of providers' decreases during a recession doesn't mean that the need for the services goes away.

In making your business more generalized you are only going on a corporate schedule what others have done on a private one-you are generalizing and putting your fingers in more pies. A corporate accountant will stretch out to encompass the company's investments and serve as a personal financial counsellor to the CEO to help the company take advantage of the opportunities offered by the stock market in light of the recession. A shuttle bus driver will extend their services to shuttle passengers all around the city.

It is all about becoming more macro and reaching out to markets that have previously been closed to you but which are now open due to a renewed need for the services you have to offer. The work is still there. The consumers are still there. The need is still there. The difference is that now you are going to be the one to ride in and scoop it up.

If you have any experience in investing you know that the key to successful investing is to maximize your profit margin (your ratio of cost to sale) as much as possible. In other words, you want to buy low and sell high!

An economic recession provides you with a unique opportunity to do that, but you have to be a savvy enough investor to know what to do with yourself when you are finished. One of the many downsides to an economic recession is that it inevitably causes the value of people's assets to drop dramatically. Houses that were worth hundreds of thousands of dollars the year before will be lucky to sell for six figures. Stock prices will be down fifty five percent.

This provides investors with the golden opportunity they have been looking for. As the recession drives the prices on these investments down lower than they did ever go under normal circumstances investors are given the chance to swoop in like a knight in shining armour, scoop up these investments and then-wait.

The biggest boon when it comes to economic recessions and business is that although it may take a few months (or years), sooner or later the economy is going to rebound. When that happens the value of all of those assets that were not worth anything during the recession is going to increase as well. At that point you are going to be sitting on a gold mine!

Chapter 8: Open yourself up to the Possibility of an International Market

Prior to the advent and mass popularity of the Internet, engaging in international commerce was a huge and difficult proposition that required you to be able to vastly undercut their domestic suppliers, provide your own means of communication and transport of your product, and most importantly, develop the right network of contacts to open doors to an industry community that will allow you to justify the investment of exporting your goods and services overseas.

And, of course, because the American economy placed such a high value on the U.S. dollar you had to convince these companies that they were justified in paying a higher price for your services than they would if they simple worked within their own borders-or at least their own continent.

There have been several events that have changed this, and which have made opening your doors to an international community not just a desirable move but a necessary one. First and foremost, the Internet has connected companies all around the globe into a single network of industry providers. Once upon a time it was inconceivable that a company in the United States would be able to write a computer program for a company in Beijing and have it in their hands by suppertime. The Internet has made that

31

possible, and made operating in an international community more lucrative and cost efficient than ever before. Unfortunately, the recessed economy in the U.S. has caused the relative value of the dollar to drop dramatically. Believe it or not, when you are considering opening your doors to the international community this is actually going to work in your favour!

A large part of the reason for the huge quantity of layoffs in the United States since the beginning of the recession is that U.S. companies have discovered a cheap labour base in companies overseas with a weaker economy. a company choosing to outsource its customer service support to the Philippines, for example, will pay those workers less than half of the minimum wage required by the U.S. government and realistically, how many Americans are going to be willing to put in the time and effort required to succeed in corporate America for minimum wage in the first place?

These employees don't have to be paid vacation, or insurance, or retirement, or any of the other "perks" that companies are offering American workers in order to ensure their loyalty and services rather than losing them to another company that's willing to provide them with that. Because of it companies are able to cut the costs of their payroll dramatically. When the company is already suffering from a reduction in profits due to an economic recession, saving those expenditures looks pretty good on their bottom line.

You can make that same principle work for you. With the value of the dollar falling there is no longer such a dramatic difference between our pay rates and the rest of the world-and if you can take that reduced dollar value and combine it with the ability to offer your customers and clients a great deal on your goods and services you can place yourself in a position not just to be able to justify your services, but to give your clients a reason to prefer them.

Top quality work at a bargain price!

Chapter 9: Recession's Effects on your Business and how to Control Them

The impact of recession can be very damaging not only to households but to businesses as well. Learn about these effects of recession and prevent your business from succumbing into its deadly claws.

1. Customer scarcity

When you have too few customers, consequently, your income suffers as well. The rising prices make customers too picky or less interested in giving you business. Existing customers may also be re-assessing their spending, which results in fewer orders for you. So what do you do? How about changing your customer acquisition techniques? Have you tried online marketing? This may not be suitable to all businesses but there's no harm in considering it. Online marketing has many forms and doing your assignment will prove to be helpful in determining which technique will benefit most your business.

2. Ridiculously high credit card debt

Inflation is likely to happen during inflation, which means your expenses can be higher than normal. If you have been relying on your credit card for payments, you now need to monitor your spending really closely. This is because losing track of your expenses can surprise you one day when you no longer have enough funds to pay off all your debt.

You do not want to have problem with your credit card because a bad rating will not be of great help when you are trying to obtain approval for loans.

3. Increase in cost of utilities

The rising price of food, electricity and gas can put a big dent to your business. This can be especially true if you run your business from a physical location. Increase in monthly bills means lower income. So how do you resolve this? There are so many ways to save money on utilities. One is to cut back on non-essentials. It the weather does not need for a full blast AC or Heather turned on, turn it off. If you can turn off the lights more often without making the business operations suffer, then do so. If you can use less expensive packaging methods or materials, please do take advantage of cheaper alternatives. Re-assess all the nooks of your business. Take a harder look to your books to get deductions. Lessen expenses in every way possible. Make the most out of technology. If you can automate parts of your business, do so. You can also hire contract workers such as virtual assistants to help you be more productive and to allow time for you to brainstorm on how to improve your business.

4. Funds gone kapoot

If you started your business using a loan, you might find yourself out of savings to fall back on if you need funds to survive the recession. To control this, have a suitable savings plan, wherein you can put in some of your income. This allows you to have a backup plan whenever the current downturn happens.

5. Low staff morale.

Slow periods mean sadder employees. Why not add incentives and create contests to boost the morale of your sales team? This is the best time to get your creative juices flowing to help motivate your employees. Having motivated employees means increased sales. So, don't be too stingy with incentives and praises.

Have you felt any of these yet? If so, what are you waiting for? Try out the suggestions on how to control the effects of recession.

Chapter 10: How your Business can survive a Recession

Almost every business will be affected by a recession. If you don't take the appropriate steps, you will have to file for bankruptcy and close. Fortunately, there are things you can do to prevent it from happening.

Focus on customer service. In any business, you have to entertain the customer so he or she will be able to buy from you. If you do this well, that person will come back and buy from you even if times are tough.

How do you focus on customer service? By retraining your staff and making sure they understand that this is the only way for your business to survive. Believe it or not, these people who you hire are the front line and if they don't do well, the customer will just go in and walk out without buying anything.

You can train them by hiring someone from the outside to handle a seminar or workshop. If this is not within your budget, do it yourself and also give them a refresher course on the products or services that you are offering.

What is at stake for them? Their jobs because you can either keep them or put them out in the street making them one of the millions of people who are now unemployed.

But this is not enough. Since you are the boss, lead by example. Work longer hours because your staff will see the amount of effort you put in and with that, nobody will have the right to complain.

If you had to borrow money to start your business, see if you can pay these loans in full. If there are other things you need to buy, see if you can get longer credit periods or better rates so large expenses can become smaller ones making it easy to manage.

Cash is hard to have during a recession. If your business does not use credit cards, now is the best time to get one because most people carry less than $500 in their wallet and have two or three pieces of plastic.

One of the hardest things to do during a recession is to cut down your profit margins. By doing this, people will be able to buy more. When things are improving, you can return these back to their normal settings.

During a recession, you must still be able to promote your business. You can do this by finding other ways to advertise like creating your own website or distributing flyers instead of paying for ads in the newspaper or billboard.

There are other ways to stay afloat during a recession and you may not have the answers so talk to other business owners and see what they are doing. Some of the steps they have taken may be applicable to your situation and you won't know that until you try.

The current recession is not only a problem in our

shores but also around the world. As you are reading this, companies are continuing to cut jobs and those who are having a hard time paying for mortgage are losing their homes. You could lose your business if you don't take drastic measures because this is the only way for you adapt with the situation and survive.

Chapter 11: Top 5 Recession-proof Businesses

In a recent poll involving 1,000 residents of the U.S., 65% said that they think that economic conditions in the country are worsening. Nearly half have already cut back on their spending and almost 20% are apprehensive about the stability of their jobs. Now that recession has finally landed, is there hope for businesses to thrive, much less survive? If starting a business in these tough times is still an option for you, here are the top 5 recession-proof businesses you might want to consider:

Health care

Regardless of the times, someone somewhere will always be in need of good, professional health service. This is an industry that has experienced some significant growth over the last few years. And it doesn't show any signs of slowing down any time soon.

If you have the resources, training, manpower and capital; becoming involved in a business that offers health services will assure you of a comfortable market. Consider businesses that focus on offering affordable preventive solutions to people, alternative health care and home health.

Food and beverages

We are not talking about pooling your hard-earned

money and starting a restaurant, although if that seems like a feasible thing to do, it just might work. However, going into the restaurant business still has its risk and a very high one.

Instead, you might consider going into a food and beverage business by focusing on offering healthier fare. These days, going into a recession is even a better excuse to eat healthy because it encourages people to cut down on their consumption and to avoid unnecessary purchases.

Consider alternative menus that are tasty and creative or specialized cafes and diners or even vegetarian eateries. Concept plus good taste are usually the best ingredients to a successful recession-proof business.

Funeral services

Yes, this is a recession-proof business, morbid as it may sound. It deals with an inevitability, which means you will never run out of customers. You could either get involved in selling services or offering related products. Cremation, which has increased in popularity in the last few years, is also a good option.

Repair services

Repair services are also recession-proof businesses. There will always be people whose kitchen sinks clog, whose air-conditioning breaks down, whose roof starts leaking or whose car suffers from overheating. What these mean is pure business opportunity, even when economic times seem shaky. And even if potential clients try to delay much-needed repair, they will still come to you for help eventually.

A caveat: many, if not all, of these businesses require specialized training, skills and equipment. However, once you have these resources, you will have access to a recession-proof business that does not only offer a potential for high margins, it is also a venture that won't require you to wait too long for a return on your investment. Provided your services are tops, it is likely that you could be in business for a very long time.

Personals

It may seem surprising but starting a business involving dating and matchmaking could help you tide the recession over. Recession or no, people will always be looking for someone special either for dating or marriage. Already, this business has hit over $650 million in sales.

As a recession-proof business, starting a personals venture could mean good profits and steady work. And no one even has to leave home. Some of the most popular companies today are those that offer online dating (Internet speed dating included) to their clients. With sufficient support, attractive and secure platforms and savvy, targeted marketing, this type of business is set to fly.

Chapter 12: Recession Proofing your Job

The first thing you want to do is protect your job. As I mentioned earlier, it's going to be the small start-up companies who haven't firmly embedded themselves into society that will feel the axe the fastest when a recession comes around. When people stop spending money, they are going to be among the first companies to stop receiving it because they simply haven't had time to dig in their roots.

If you work for a company that is going to feel very little effects as a result of a recession you have very little to worry about. Regardless of what company you work for, however, now is a great time to start making yourself indispensable. It is simple fact that the employees that are the first to go when a company starts making lay-offs are the ones who are not deemed to be important enough to stay-sort of like acceptable loss in a war zone. Those employees have to go in order for the company to thrive.

Making yourself an indispensible part of your company is the first step toward recession proofing your job. Even companies that are cutting down on their staff are going to hesitate to get rid of individuals who are essential to their company's daily operations. This would be an excellent time to consider volunteering to take on extra work or become more actively involved in long term projects or contracts.

If you can, involve yourself in several projects your company is working on (obviously without stretching yourself so thin that you can no longer do your job to the best of your ability). The more pies you have your fingers in, the more hesitant management will be to let you go. In times of recession companies may be cutting back on their employees, but that doesn't mean that they are going to be able to cut back on the amount of work they have to do. It just means that that work is going to be re-delegated. If you are already actively involved in several ongoing projects the company will find it much easier to simply accord you extra responsibilities on these projects than to attempt to bring a new man up to speed.

A heads up this is NOT the time to attempt to apply for a promotion or a transfer, however promising that transfer may be. The minute you accept this type of move you become the new man on the block, and immediately become more vulnerable when the time comes to go through and decide who will go and who will stay.

Right before the string of layoffs in 2007 due to the termination of numerous government contracts one well known government agency had just opened a new department and moved a large quantity of their oldest and most experienced employees on over. Despite the fact that many of these employees had put in more time with the company than the management they were working under, because their department was "new" they were among the first to lose their jobs when the company started laying off.

Attitude counts a LOT. A recent article published by Fortune magazine stated that when management is trying to decide who will stay and who will go, often attitude and the employee's ability to boost morale is as strong a determining factor as their ability to do their job.

When the going gets tough, the tough have to get going. Remember, companies trying to stay on top during a recession are going to have higher expectations of their employees than ever before. The only way these employees are going to be able to meet those expectations is if they are able to keep their morale high.

An employee who drags that morale down is going to quickly find themselves looking for another job.

Just in Case...

Hopefully the economic recession is not going to impact your job but that doesn't mean you shouldn't take precautions. You don't want to wait until you are holding your pink slip in hand and wondering how you are going to make next month's mortgage payment to start looking around for another job and you don't want to wait until you need something from them to touch base with your old bosses and co-workers and your friends and acquaintances that might be able to offer you work when the going gets rough.

Network

It is all about networking. If you know anything about real estate you know "location, location, location" is every agent's mantra. (Right after "Buy low and sell high".) A piece of property that is within easy walking distance to schools, grocery stores and public transportation is going to be far more desirable than one that is miles away from everything, no matter how beautiful the location. The same thing applies to you when the time comes for you to find a job. That house in the middle of everything is going to sell much more quickly, and you, in the middle of a huge network of friends and potential employers, are going to be able to find work much more rapidly.

If you have kept in touch with your bosses and associates, both past and present, you will not only probably already know who is hiring and who is not; you may have the inside track when it comes to finding another job.

If you wait to get in touch with them until you have been laid off, however, you are going to find yourself struggling. They are going to know that the only reason you are contacting them is because you are hoping to get a job, and they are going to look at you unfavourably not only because you are willing to use your friends that way in the first place, but that you would be caught so unprepared. They are going to be far more concerned with their own affairs at that point than they are about yours.

Be Visible

No matter how much you have been looking forward to spending the next three weeks onboard a Carnival cruise ship, when your company starts making budget cuts is absolutely, positively not the time to take an extended vacation. You can't show someone how valuable you are if you're not there! When they sit down to review employee records and someone asks, "Hey, where's…?" and someone else answers, "Oh, he is on vacation..."-well, you can imagine where that conversation is going to go.

That doesn't mean you have to deprive yourself of a well earned week away from the office. If you tend to take your vacations in bulk (disappearing for two to three weeks at a time) this is a fine opportunity to spread those vacations out a little-a week here, three or four days there will give you a break while still keeping you in the corporate eye. No one expects you to work yourself to death (and if they do, they will never admit it in public). You just don't want to take that vacation at a time when taking a little break could turn into an extended one-as in, permanently.

Remember, the average recession in the past only lasts eleven months, however this one is lasting longer. Giving up your extended vacation for a single year is a small price to pay for keeping your job…and your pay cheque and your pension and your health insurance…You get the picture. You can always enjoy that month in Paradise next year.

Chapter 13: Offer Suggestions on Ways to Save the Company Money

In the middle of a recession even companies that have historically been very employee oriented are going to have to shift their focus from creating a great place to work to creating a way to trim the fat off of their budget while continuing to remain competitive in the marketplace and lure in consumers who would otherwise prefer to spend their money elsewhere. This is going to be their top priority!

Because saving money while still continuing to make money is going to be a vital part of the company's continued existence (and because it can be so difficult to do in an economy that thrives on the idea that you have to spend money to make money) an employee that can help them achieve that goal is going to instantly become one of the company's greatest assets. You don't dispose of assets that are generating a tangible return in the middle of a recession.

Employees that can help a company move forward while at the same time preserving their bottom line are going to be worth their weight in gold in the eyes of the corporate bigwigs, and you can guarantee that these individuals are not going to be the ones standing in the unemployment line!

Can't come up with any clever suggestions to help your company cut its costs? Here are some ideas to get you started:

1. Trim the fat on the office supplies. You did be amazed at what the average office spends in pencils, paper and folders a month!

2. Find a way to go through and lower production costs without losing quality.

3. If you can discover a way to decrease the cost of transporting your products you will instantly become your office's golden child! The increase in the cost of oil (and subsequently gasoline) has spurred an almost ludicrous increase in the cost of transporting goods, which in turn has forced companies to raise the price of their goods, which in turn is leading to the loss of business in the recessed economy as customers complain about the increase in the price of goods and take their business elsewhere.

4. New employee perks. Companies that don't offer their employees any perks whatsoever usually don't have employees for very long. Even the most unconcerned companies generally host a Christmas party or other annual event for the people that keep the wheels of their company turning, as well as a steady stream of incentives throughout the year to keep morale high and encourage greater productivity. If you can think of a steady stream of employee (and client) perks that will require the company to part with less money out of pocket you will be well on your

way to establishing yourself as an invaluable member of your company's team.

Keep Your Skills Up to Date It doesn't matter what industry you happen to be in, sweeping changes in supply, demand and technology are going to require you to stay up to date with what is happening in the field. If you have simply coasted along up until this point, grandfathering your way along while your co-workers went back to school, attended certification classes and furthered their education; you are going to find yourself in a sticky situation in the middle of a recession.

When preparing to weather a recession companies are going to consider the long term outlook for their company rather than the short term, which means that their priority when considering which employees are going to go and which ones are going to stay is finding high quality workers that are going to be able to help the company keep pushing forward in changing times.

This is one of those times when that insignificant little piece of paper helps. Unless you have worked extensively with the technologies or programs that your company specializes in and know it inside, outside and backwards without the benefit of taking a class or two to show you how to do it, you are going to find yourself pushed out of the way in favour of a younger employee who has taken the time to expand their horizons.

Education counts. If you haven't already, take this opportunity to see what kind of tuition reimbursement your company offers and what certifications are available in your field.

THERE IS NO POSSIBLE WAY TAKING THIS STEP WILL HURT YOU!

Ideally, furthering your education will make your boss see what a valuable asset you are to your company and keep your job secure during these trying times; however, if your company still decides to let you go these certifications are going to look great on a resume when you go to find another job. Companies love ambitious, motivated employees as much as they love well educated, experienced ones, and by taking the initiative and obtaining these certifications without any nudging from your boss you will be proving yourself to be both.

Chapter 14: Keep Looking

Walking around advertising the fact that you are looking for another job never endears you to employers, but secretly doing so in the face of an economic recession and a possible lay-off is just good sense. By continuing to job hunt even though you already have a job you will be accomplishing several things:

1. First and foremost, you will be able to keep a weather eye on what is available on the market and with whom. Although you don't want to be the new kid on the block when companies are looking to start cutting their payroll, if a favourable position becomes available with a company that stands a very good chance of weathering a recession while your company is almost guaranteed to cut your job in the next eight to twelve weeks, you did be a fool not to snatch at the opportunity. It might mean taking a little bit of a chance, but the bottom line is that by doing so you will also be setting yourself up to be gainfully employed while your co-workers are standing in the unemployment line.

2. Secondly, you will be preparing yourself for change. If you have ever seen the children's video Kung Fu Panda you will remember the infamous words of the immortal Master Oogway-"There is no good news or bad news. There is only news." The determining

factor in whether news is viewed as good or bad is precisely that-how you view it.

If you look at a recession and a possible layoff as a stimulus for change (change that you can be prepared for if you make the effort) then you will have no problem when it comes time to say goodbye to the old and hello to the new. On the other hand, if you are still rooted in the thought that the world is going to come to an end if you lose your job and have to go hunting for another one you are going to find yourself mired in confusion and misery when you are handed that pink slip a mucky place that is going to hold on to you until the consequences become all too obvious.

Chapter 15: If you do get Laid Off

"When one door closes, another opens; but we often look so long and so regretfully upon the closed door that we do not see the one which has opened for us."

Michael John Wilson

It started off as a regular morning. You got up, had your daily fix of caffeinated Columbian goodness, wolfed down a bagel sandwich from Dunkin Donuts on the road and strolled into your office with your briefcase in one hand and cell phone in the other-only to have the boss come by and tell you (without nearly enough regret) that you have been laid off and you only have two weeks to find another job.

Unfortunately, hundreds of people are going to find themselves in this position as the economy continues to take a downturn. No matter how normal it may be, an economic recession is going to take a toll on its residents. At this point, you are going to have two options. You can choose to flip your lid, like Milton in the movie Office Space, clinging desperately to your belief that the company could never really let you go because they can't possibly function without you. Or you can choose to sadly pack up your stapler, your calculator and your top secret stash of Werther's Originals that you have been hiding in your desk since last Christmas and move on.

Studies show that Generation X and Y'ers entering today's workplace have a far better chance of riding out an economic recession without suffering a major blow to their self esteem or their financial security than the baby boomers. Why? Because the thought of spending their entire adult lives working for the same company never occurred to them. They expect to switch jobs several times in their careers, hopping from opportunity to opportunity as it presented itself, and are more likely to look at a layoff as an opportunity to round out their resume in other areas than their older co-workers.

This is who you want to be. You want to be that employee that looks at that pink slip and thinks, "Hmmm, maybe I will finally get the chance to try my hand at teaching college/coaching soccer/writing the next great American novel/etc." No, the next year might not help you make great strides toward who you want to be when you grow up. Yes, you might find yourself living hand to mouth for a couple of months while you adapt to a new lifestyle and wait for the chance to slip back into the industry you intend to call your own.

The point is, one way or another, this too shall pass. Sooner or later the economy is going to kick back up, and you will be able to get on with the plans you had when you first took that job you were so worried about losing. The question is how do you intend to spend that time in between?

Do you want to spend it constantly sweating and worrying about how the recession is going to affect your financial situation? Or do you want to be able to grab the opportunity presented to you with both hands and say "Not a single second of a single minute of a single hour of a single day passed me by that I wasn't looking for that open door!"

Chapter 16: Career Shift During Recession

One of the ways to cope with recession is considering a career shift. Not too many likes the idea of changing career plans during a downturn. However, if you have already felt the effect of recession say you've been laid off, why not give a different career path a chance, right? It may not have quickly crossed your mind to prioritize job security when choosing a job. However, whether you are choosing your first job or making a switch, it can be helpful, particularly during our present economic situation. Indeed, no job is 100% secure. But there are some industries that have workers feeling more confident that even if they get fired, the demand is so great that finding another job would be very easy.

So how do you choose a career that is right for you during a recession? Here are some recession-proof careers that are worthy of consideration:

Education

There is a great shortage of teachers. No matter how down the economy is, teachers will always be in-demand. Children will continue to go to school. Also, lots of unemployed adults may decide to further their education. Although teaching is not one of the highest-paid careers there is, making only about $30,000 to $45,000 a year, people will still settle for a career that does not earn more because they are tired of being unemployed for a long time. This is especially true for those who would want to try something new anyway or those who despise the roller-coaster ride that a corporate life offers.

Healthcare

Job hunters with Information Technology background are said to be a good fit to the healthcare industry particularly nursing. This is because nursing is an information-driven career and, it is one useful career during a recession because healthcare is an industry that does not usually get affected during these times.

Auditing

Auditors are also usually unaffected by downturns. In a recession, individuals and firms are more probably doing their best to get more deductions. More people are monitoring their books, so the demand for auditors or accountants is much greater.

Energy and Utilities

Energy consumers may cut back, but the consumption will not stop. The same with utilities, people will still light their homes. So, jobs like maintenance and utility administration prove to be more stable than others during a recession.

Pharmaceuticals

As long as physicians prescribe drugs, people are still going to take them. This means that if you are working as a pharmacist or as a quality assurance analyst in pharmaceutical laboratory, you are in good hands.

Military

Since the military is always hiring, particularly during wartime, during a recession soldiers will not be that affected, unless you are unfortunate to be in the military right now in the UK. Serving the military also means that most of your living expenses will be covered.

Security

Recession does not stop crime. With the increase in layoffs, more people are considering robbing banks and doing other crimes. So, the need for security workers becomes greater.

Environmental Sciences

The convenient truth is that the eco-friendly trend is not going anywhere. This means that choosing a career in environment-care-related industries can be a good career choice.

Government

Working for the government can be one of your best choices during this downturn. This is because many stable jobs can be found in the federal government. The government will not cease from functioning even during crisis, however you do not want to be working for UK government right now because the new UK Government have just announce massive layoff of Government workers.

With that variety of career choices, it will not be that difficult to find one that will save you from this economic situation.

Chapter 17: Finding Recession Proof Jobs

Recession can be a very stubborn thing. Once it drops by, it can take a while for it to fade away and disappear. However, that doesn't mean that we should simply sit back and let it overcome us. It can, after all, wreck havoc on our finances and personal lives. In these tough times, finding a job already seems improbable just imagine being in the market for jobs that are not affected by recession. But take heart. There is still hope yet.

Here are top 6 tips for finding recession-proof jobs:

Look for jobs in secure industries. If you have read the news by now, trying to get a job in an auto plant is like trying to get on an elevator that is going down and you are trying to go up. The same is true if you are trying to get a leg in real estate.

Instead of wasting your time trying to join an industry that is experiencing some bad times, try to set your sights on industries that have remained stable or are experiencing growths. These include:
1.   Health care (nursing, care-giving, special care, medicine, physical therapy and other support manpower)
2.   Law enforcement
3.   Information Technology (network administration, software design and development)

4. Support Services (customer service, administrative assistance)
5. Sales and business development (product management, retail and wholesale)
6. Engineering
7. Education (teaching, school administration and other related support services)

Boost your resume.

If an employer sees nothing promising or exciting in your resume, they won't think twice about throwing your piece in the trash bin. Before you try to hook a recession-proof job, consider revamping your resume right now. Take a copy of your latest and review it. If your resume is several months old, there is a high likelihood that it needs a makeover.

Focus on accomplishments.

A common error among job hunters is detailing their job descriptions in their resumes. Although this is helpful in establishing their work experience, it may not always give the prospective employer a good idea of what you can do. Emphasize on the results that you have produced instead.

Adapt your resume.

Typing out and printing a generic resume is a huge mistake. Generic is average, which means that you have very little to help you stand out from the crowd. If you want a recession-proof job, make sure your resume is something that your employers will find attractive.

Consider the industry you are targeting. If the job calls for someone who has a strong sales experience, emphasize your sales background. If the job calls for someone who had been involved directly in marketing and promotions, show your qualifications in these departments. The more relevant your resume says you are, the better you will be at landing a recession-proof job.

Expand your reach.

Other than advertised job vacancies, consider other venues for finding recession-proof jobs. Look for trade magazines, papers, clubs and associations. You could also tap your network of professionals in the same field.

Get further education.

In tough times, you ought to arm yourself with tougher credits. One is by obtaining additional training or education. Getting certified or expanding your professional qualifications will help make you a more desirable hire.

Recession-proof jobs are usually the most popular among job hunters who are probably considering the same strategies as you right now. It's likely that for every recession-proof job that is available out there, there are thousands of other job hunters out to get it. If you have better qualifications courtesy of better training and experience (in case you have had hands-on education or internship), you will come out as the best, most capable candidate.

Chapter 18: Recession Proof your Home

Anti-Recession Tips: Simple Ways for Home Makers to Not Feel Recession's Wrath

Recession, for the uninitiated, is the decline of the economy. It is a widespread decline in the Gross Domestic Product, employment, and trade, which lasts from 6 months couple of years. One of its usual effects is running out of funds because of the high prices of commodity and the increase in unemployment rate. So, if you are running a household, how do you make sure the impact of recession will not be too much to bear for your family? Here are some anti-recession tips that you can find useful during these hard times:

Grow Your Own Fresh Produce.

If you have been relying on the supermarkets for your daily meals, it's high time to consider growing your own food. What can be better than taking advantage of your green thumb to avoid having to buy fruits and vegetables? If you are renting, growing vegetables and herbs in pots, also known as container gardening, can be useful. Mint, sage, rosemary, basil and thyme are great herbs for container gardening. If you do not have enough time, opt for low maintenance vegetables. Examples of low maintenance vegetables include garlic, onions, turnips, cabbage, leeks and kale. Now if you have a bigger backyard, growing your own fruits can be fruitful (pun not intended). Although this might require longer time since fruit trees can take at least about two years to yield crops. You can also do better in keeping a wide variety of your fruits and vegetables through trading with your neighbour's grown fruit trees, vegetables and herbs.

Make Your Own Meal.

If you have the time, learning how to bake can be one great way to spend your free time. Aside from saving money, it can also be one fun way to relieve your stress. Fast food restaurants can be very tempting but if you have the skills (or not, since you can learn to cook), then why not prepare your own food from your own grown fruits and vegetables and home-baked bread. If you think your skills are too limited, the Internet offers gazillions of simple recipes that even kids can make. Make your own coffee and you can also brew your own beer if you want.

Improve your grocery shopping habits.

With the right shopping attitude, you can reduce unnecessary cost. You can prevent yourself from succumbing into impulse buying. You can do this by creating a list of items to buy before going to the supermarket. One tip is to not go to the grocery to shop when you are hungry. Yes, hunger causes you to buy items you do not need. Buying all the items you need in one go can help avoid using gas for unnecessary trip and also get rids of temptation. Also, before you unloading your cart, check again which items you can do without. You will be surprised that there are just so many of the items that you picked up that you do not really need.

Cut back on non-essentials.

You like soda? You like steak? But do you like to survive the recession? Then, cut on soda, meat and other non-essentials. You do not have to stop drinking soda or eating meat. But if you will only compute how much you can save without consuming any of these as often as you used to, you will see that it's enough to tide you over.

Chapter 19: Buying Properties During Recession

Considering the fact that it was real estate that started the ball rolling toward economic disaster in the first place, it is rather ironic that it is in real estate that investors really have the opportunity to capitalize on economic recession and turn what could be a potentially devastating economic downturn into a major opportunity for profit. Why? Because real estate is one of the major assets whose value is plummeting in the face of a never ending stream of foreclosures and bankruptcies, and it is real estate whose value is guaranteed to go up when the recession is over.

Think about it. Will there ever come a time when real estate isn't a desperately needed asset?

Absolutely not! People are always going to need places to live and place to work, and because of that there will always be a need for real estate. That is why a huge percentage of entrepreneurs are jumping on board the real estate bandwagon to grow wealth and increase their net worth. It is one of the only markets out there that is guaranteed to never become obsolete!

A major contributor to the current economic crises and the fact that major players like Freddie Mac and Fannie Mae are going under as huge number of people defaulting on their mortgages. When the concept of interest only loans and other special programs designed to help those individuals who otherwise would never qualify for any type of mortgage purchase a home first came out everyone thought it was a great idea-and in many ways it was. It placed the power to purchase property in the hands of people who otherwise wouldn't have the ability to do it, and it sent banks into raptures as more and more people came to them for assistance in buying or refinancing their first home.

Then reality struck. The bottom line is that many of these homeowners weren't able to get a mortgage in the first place because they didn't have the means to repay it, and while for some people the programs worked like they were supposed to (interest only loans for first time home buyers still trying to find their niche in the workplace, for example, who later became responsible citizens and were able to shoulder the increased burden of their mortgage payment when the time came to begin making payments on the principle) others just found themselves going further and further into debt.

Skip ahead six months to a year, and suddenly a huge percentage of these homeowners are defaulting on their loans. Banks are foreclosing left and right, and they are struggling to get rid of these properties as quickly as possible to get them off their records. Each property goes to a foreclosure auction, where it sells for less than it would have outright at fair market value, and the bank barely reclaims its investment.

Fast forward a little further and suddenly huge quantity of people are out of jobs as the economy continues to slide. You have a huge pool of homeowners whose income, once strong and steady courtesy of major manufacturers and/or the United States government, is now no longer sufficient to meet their financial obligations. They can't pay their mortgages that they took out when their resources were more than sufficient to meet their needs, and the bank has to foreclose on those properties as well.

The real estate market is plunged into chaos, property values are falling rapidly in an attempt to stem the tide of destruction sweeping from coast to coast, and clever investors are rubbing their hands together in glee.

During an economic recession homebuyers simply aren't buying homes. They are pumping their money into other things. This inspires desperate homeowners to put their homes on the market for far less than they are actually worth in an attempt to make a sale that will be adequate to allow them to pay off the bank and be free of the mortgage default hanging over their head.

Enter the real estate investor. They soothingly placate the homeowner, assuring them that of course they are there to put everything to right. They contact the bank to let them know that they will be purchasing the property so that the bank can halt any legal foreclosure proceedings they may have initiated, and then they pay the happy homeowner and send them on their way, holding the deed to the property. This process is repeated over and over again every day during an economic recession, particularly once that recession has begun to have a positive (or negative, depending on how you want to look at it) effect on the value of the housing market. It is not at all unusual for a clever investor to find a homeowner who has built up some equity in their home and who will gladly sell it for a fraction of the cost it would go for on the open market.

In dollars and cents, it means that it's not at all unheard of for an investor to purchase a $350,000 home for under $200,000 during an economic recession. The value of the property has fallen so far and the homeowner is so far behind on their financial obligations that they are willing to let the property go for a song just to dodge the stigma of bankruptcy or foreclosure that would otherwise be lingering over their heads.

After the investor has the property in his hands he has a choice. He can either choose to turn right around and sell it to a rehabber or private homeowner. He can hold on to it, rehab it himself and rent it out (since affordable rental property will be highly in demand in the face of the rapidly failing housing market, with hundreds of families ousted from their homes and left to find another place to live), or simply sit and hold on to it.

As an investor during an economic recession it's vitally important that you understand the basic framework of a recession. THE RECESSION IS NOT GOING TO LAST FOREVER! Sooner or later the economy is going to start getting back to normal, and when it does the value on your investment is going to rise back up. That $200,000 home is suddenly going to sell for $350,000 again- more if it happens to be in an area that sees a tremendous boom as a result of the ending depression.

That means that if you can afford to do it, the best thing you can do at this point is play a waiting game. You know the value of your property is only going to rise, and if you rehab it while you're waiting you can watch the value rise even more. Let's take that $350,000 house and use it for an example again. Let's assume for a moment that the house is sitting on a lightly wooded lot with a big backyard an easy commute away from a major, booming industrial area.

Let's also assume that the industrial area saw a major boom as a result of the ending recession, and that because of that boom property values in the area were jerked back up. That house that was worth $350,000 and sold for $200,000 is suddenly worth $400,000; however, while they were waiting for the end of the recession the homeowner also took the opportunity to rehab the property, doing some landscaping, adding a pool and a spa room and installing all new plumbing and appliances.

Suddenly that property that the investor bought for $200,000 and invested $40,000 to fix up is worth over $500,000. Even with the additional $40,000 investment for the rehabilitation the real estate purchaser is going to walk away with a tidy $100,000 in their pocket-more than many executives make in two years, and all because they were clever enough to take advantage of an opportunity when one presented itself on the back of an economic recession. If you are looking for a way to take advantage of the recession and you have the time and the money to do it, I strongly recommend real estate. The good thing about real estate is that if you know the ins and outs of the business you can enjoy a return from this career whether you choose to think in the short term or the long term-although, for the sake of this book, I'm going to encourage you to put at least a little bit of thought into the long term.

Remember, long term when you are talking about an economic recession isn't the same as when you're talking about the long term anywhere else. A recession usually lasts less than a year, however this one has last longer. A year's worth of stockpiling for a lifetime's worth of profit. Hmmm...

Chapter 20: Buying Properties During Recession: Do's and Don'ts

When you are going shopping for real estate in the middle of an economic recession you can pretty much guarantee that whatever you purchase, you're going to be able to make a profit. There are certain parts of the country that take a little longer to be affected when a recession strikes, but sooner or later every place is going to start to feel the pinch-which means you can basically stick a pin in the map when you're trying to decide where you want to make your investment.

Of course, just because you can make a profit just about anywhere doesn't mean that you shouldn't take measures to maximize that profit. If you were sitting in the middle of a giant room of sweets that were yours for the taking absolutely free, would you go for the Godiva chocolate or the M&Ms? When you have the choice between a property that you're going to make a minimal investment on and a property that you will make an incredible profit on when the economy starts rising up again, go for the property that's going to bring you the best return!

Where are you going to find the best deals? Urban properties and homes in the suburbs of these urban areas are always more highly in demand than those that require a lengthy commute to get to lives essentials. Homes in the suburbs of Washington, D.C. are going to sell for a greater profit (and much more quickly) than a home in a small town like Rexville, NY. (Don't worry if you've never heard of it most of the rest of the world hasn't either!)

When you first begin investing it's usually recommended that you pick a property close to home, where you know the neighbourhood, the general ambiance and, most importantly, what sells! If you choose to do your own rehab this is particularly important, as there are many areas in the country that are particularly prized for their historical value and which will bring a much lower return on your investment if they have been stripped and decked out in the latest style than if they did been carefully restored. An experienced rehabber will know this. A beginning investor will not.

Other factors you may want to take into consideration before closing the deal are:
1. The quality of the neighbourhood. Unfortunately, all urban areas have their slums. An area with a high crime rate, a wide-spread amount of graffiti and property damage, regular drug activity and daily visits from the police is going to be much less desirable to a prospective buyer than a home situation in a nicer part of town, where they can safely allow their children to step out the front door without having to worry that they won't come home.

2. The condition of the house. There have been many, many investors that have plunged right in to the world of real estate and rehabilitation

82

and bought a handyman's special only to discover that by the time they got done paying for the repairs to the property the profit margin was considerably less than what they were hoping for and what they would have made investing in a property that needed a little less work.

3. Before you commit to buying a property, take the time to have the home inspected carefully. Certain factors, such as a leaky roof, faulty foundation, termites and extensive mould, are going to be both difficult and expensive to fix. Unless you can quite literally get the property for a song, justifying the amount of time and expense you are going to put into the restoration project, it may be best to allow that one to pass you by.

4. What you plan to do with it afterwards. This is probably the biggest factor when it comes to real estate investing, because what you plan to do with the property after you purchase it makes all the difference when you are determining what types of properties are suitable and what are not. If you are planning on rehabilitating a property, then reselling it as a single family residence, purchasing a small ranch house on the edge of the city may be a perfectly profitable proposition. You'll likely be able to sell the property for more than you paid for it and justify the investment.

On the other hand, if you are planning on renting the property out you are going to want to investigate the current rental rates of the neighbourhood before you'll be able to determine the success of the investment with any degree of accuracy. There are some areas where income based housing drives the average rental price of the neighbourhood down, which is good news for renters but could result in major inconvenience for the investor who has paid hundreds of thousands of dollars for a property that they are only going to be able to rent for a couple hundred dollars a month.

The moral of my story! Take the time to carefully consider your options and do your homework before closing the deal, no matter how appealing that deal may be.

Of course, if you've been investing in real estate for the past ten years none of this is news to you!

Experienced investors who are familiar with things like market trends and identifying weaknesses in potential properties will find the buffet of low priced real estate spread out before them a tempting proposition, and reaching beyond their immediate demographic boundaries may offer a new wealth of possibilities for tremendous profit gain.

Just remember that investing during a recession is a slightly different proposition than investing when the economy is booming. You are going to hear me say this over and over again; because it can't be emphasized enough-when you are investing in real estate during a recession you are investing in the long term. Many of today's real estate investors have made their fortune in the market by taking advantage of today's "Now, now, now!" mindset and investing in and disposing of real estate in a very brief amount of time. When the economy is strong it is not at all unusual for an experienced investor to be able to purchase and flip a property within the space of a week, experienced rehabbers in a month of less.

Any property that you invest in during a recession may remain in your possession for several months before you are able to realize a maximum return, because the whole point of investing during a recession is to purchase an asset at the lowest price possible and sell it when the economy goes back up. It's rare for the experienced investor to find themselves in this situation, but it's entirely possible to spread yourself too thin when the temptation of pages upon pages of available property was just too much to resist. Suddenly they are responsible not only for the amount they have paid for the initial investment to purchase the property in the first place, but for the taxes, rehabilitation and maintenance required to keep it maintained and prepare it for sale.

Try to limit yourself with a realistic expectation of what you can afford in the long term. If as the recession continues you find you have more than enough capital in hand to pick up a couple more properties you always have that option, but disposing of a property you can no longer afford during a recession can be more difficult than taking a submarine and going diving for Atlantis which is the reason that investing in real estate during a recession is so lucrative to begin with.

Don't come undone with your own expectations.

Determining whether you have gotten yourself a good deal in buying real estate, or simply just about anything, depends on your priorities. We all differ in a priority that is a fact. So if you did like to make sure you satisfy yourself, get your own expectations in check. Creating a checklist can help you here. Finding a property to buy with a checklist handy can greatly facilitate the process.

Don't be too you-you-you.

Sure, you were advised to know your priorities and to create a checklist to boot. However, flexibility can also get you a long way. Be objective with your judgments and take a hard look at the property you are planning to buy. Think hard and see if you are actually being too choosy to the point of being impractical. Would you like fancy or functional? Is it comfy or elegant? How about trying to meet in the middle? Have you asked for suggestions from experts, family or friends with experience? Do they agree with you? Although you do not need to wipe your slate clean and accommodate all their opinions, are your expectations realistic enough and what about your budget? Remember it is recession.

Don't be over-confident during a real estate recession.

Many think that since it is recession, they can just buy and buy and buy properties. Although many property sellers are usually on the lower part of the scale during these times, not all deals are the best ones. You still need to be as careful as ever in purchasing real estate.

Before pursuing a short sale...

Many would pursue a short sale trying to grab a good deal. However, before you buy a property with a price that seems too low for the location, asking your agent to investigate if it is a short sale won't hurt. This is important since you should not just make an offer on a pre-foreclosure, short sale property.

Beware during recession since there are not too many fish in the sea i.e., properties to buy. Home sellers do know that during a recession, they may not be able to sell their properties for a better price. This means that they would have to wait longer to put their home out on the market. There may be properties for sale, but they get bought quicker, too. It would be helpful if you are prepared enough to make a purchase without dilly-dallying if you really are into it.

Recession or not...

Your decision should not be clouded in buying a property. Always shop for the lowest price, which fortunately is more attainable during recession for buyers. However, do not forget that the lowest-priced property is not necessarily the best one.

In summary, there are some advantages to buying a

home during recession. However, if you do not really have the budget or are not that well-educated in the real estate industry, do not feel pressured to jump in.

Chapter 21: Tips for Effective Tax and Personal Anti-recession Steps

Ask an economist to define recession for you and chances are they will tell you that it is a state of the economy where it declines for at least 6 months. But that is just a pretty, picture-book definition. Recession can affect not just cities and countries; it can also affect individuals and families on a more personal level. To help you implement tax and personal anti-recession steps, here are things you can do:

Start saving. Now.

If you have a nest egg stashed somewhere, good for you. Boost it with more savings. If you don't, it is time to start immediately. Implement tax and personal savings steps in order to fight the effects of recession.

Cut back on spending immediately.

If you think you need everything you buy, gather your last few weeks' worth of receipts and rate each item according to necessity. Chances are there are a few things there that you will realize now that you didn't really have to buy.

If you see the same pattern in most of your receipts, that's a sign that you ought to cut back on your expenses and seriously implement a budget or spending plan. You could, for example, cancel gym memberships and take up running or home exercises instead, buy items on sale instead of at regular prices and put off any large purchases like cars, TVs, video equipment, furniture, etc.

Take big chunks out of your debt.

Your debt can get you down and it will not hesitate to do the same thing to your credit score. During a recession, a bad credit rating is just not something you want to have. If you have debts in some form (loans, credit cards, mortgage, etc.), try to pay off as much of your debt as possible. The earlier you do this, the better it will be for your finances.

Clearing your debts is an excellent anti-recession step because it helps save you money in terms of interest. It will also give you peace of mind and the personal satisfaction of being in charge.

Consider investing? Ask a professional.

An experienced financial adviser can help you understand the kind of options you have, given your own resources and the type of risks you are willing to take. Recession can make investing much more of a challenge, particularly for the uninitiated. That is why you will need all the help you can get in order to find the best places where to put your money in.

Know your deductibles.

Review your tax code for the types of items that you

can include in your deductibles. Remember that not all expenses can be used as deductions. Only if you can prove them 'ordinary and necessary' will the tax man consider them.

Keep all receipts for deductions.

Audit or no audit, it pays to have documents that support your tax claims, especially if they refer to deductions. Get organized regarding your files, particularly those that pertain to your business or work. Keep things where you can readily access them and use for reference later.

Consider leasing your business vehicle.

If you want to give yourself better tax performance, a good anti-recession tip to follow is to lease that car of yours. This will help get you better deductions compared to what you will receive if you purchased the vehicle.

When in doubt, always refer to a professional.

The personal anti-recession tips you obtain will usually work seamlessly but some steps involving taxes might have certain limitations. Before implementing these steps, you might want to consult a basic taxation guide or see an accountant or bookkeeper. They can guide you on what you can and should do based on your own unique circumstances.

92

Chapter 22: Saving Money and Recession

Saving Money During a Recession: Mission Impossible?

Recession is a word that fills people with dread and bad visions. It is a time people consider bad for finances, a time capable of magically shrinking a money value overnight. It also automatically increases the cost of basic living. And where money is a huge concern, people always ask, 'Can I still save for real during a recession?' The answer is: of course you can. You just need to be wise and creative about the whole thing. Here are ways how:

Plan your purchases.

By planning your purchases, you are effectively planning your expenses. This will help eliminate the danger of impulse buying and unnecessary spending. Try to look at the bigger picture when it comes to your basic needs.

Plan for a week's worth of groceries, for example, so you will have an idea of which items you truly need (and want) and which items you can do away with. To make sure that you maximize your planning efforts, consider incorporating items on sale into your planning. If there are foods on sale that week, for example, why not plan your week's menu using what's currently on slashed down prices?

Implement the 'B' word.

Budget, that is. If you want to be able to save money during a recession, learn to discipline yourself and your family. Using your plan as a reference, come up with a weekly or monthly budget and then stick to it. If you must overshoot it, you should have a very good reason to do so. Otherwise, don't spend.

Keep an eye out for bargains and discounts.

Learn to monitor stores for seasonal sales. You will save a lot of money by buying items on sale than in their regular prices. During a recession, that is considered wise spending. Check out store or newspaper ads and don't be shy about asking for cheaper alternatives, getting store rebates or using discount coupons. Consider buying at discount stores as well. Each dollar you don't pay is a dollar you save.

Buy in bulk.

If there are items in your house that are often in use (paper towels, canned beans, yoghurt, etc.), consider buying in bulk. Many stores offer items in packs, which means you will save money in the long run if you buy them instead of paying for individual items.

Put off bigger purchases.

A good rule of thumb is, if you can't afford it, don't buy it. If, for example, you have enough money for a down payment on a new LCD TV but will have to borrow money off your credit card just to tide you over for the next few weeks, it would be really insane to make a purchase. Wait until you can truly, comfortably afford something. The worst you can do during a recession is not just failing to get money saved but also going into debt.

Practice prevention, not cure.

If you look closely, there are many things you do in your home that are siphoning precious dollars from your wallet. Simple steps such as repairing and maintaining your home and appliances, using more efficient equipment and cutting down on unnecessary consumption can do wonders for your wallet and piggy bank. And what better way to treat a recession than to be prudent?

Earn extra money.

If, after all your efforts, the money you have saved is still not enough, don't let recession get the better of you. There are times when your efforts are just not sufficient, mostly because you don't earn enough. Instead of asking for a raise that might never occur or waiting for a promotion to drop on your lap, consider finding other means with which to earn (and save) money.

Consider getting a part-time job, work extra hours, do selling on the side or offer your skills as a freelancer. The extra income you earn, along with your recession-powered money-saving plan, will help you make enough until after the tough times are over.

Chapter 23: Recession proof your Family's Entertainment - Low Cost Ways to Have Fun

Recession does not mean boredom for your family. You do not have to slump down at home trying to sleep the recession away when you can still have fun without having to spend too much. Here are some ways to keep your family entertained without putting a big dent to your budget.

Grow a Green Thumb – Low Cost Way to Have Fun and Have Food

Gardening is one of the most productive and yet less-costly ways to entertain oneself. If you have the kids helping, you can double the fun. Just as long as you do not use high-maintenance, which are also usually expensive plants, you can have a ball growing vegetables and fruits that you can also use to make your own meals. This means more savings for your family!

Watch your Local Sports Team – Inexpensive Way to Support your Local Team

Kids enjoy watching sports. Support your local sports team by adding yourself and your kid as part of its seated cheering squad.

Go to community events – Low Cost Activity to Enjoy: Your Neighbourhood's Events

Your local colleges, city bulletin boards, newspaper listings, and libraries usually post special entertainment events that you can attend for free.

Host a Garage Sale – Fun and Inexpensive Way to Earn Extra Income

It's high time to get rid of your old bags that only gather dust in your closet. And what better way to get rid of it than to sell it in a garage sale. A garage sale is not just a way to earn you extra money; it can be highly entertaining, too. Getting the whole family to participate, from gathering the items, pricing and selling them can be a whole bunch of fun.

Backyard Camping – Go Cheap, Local and Fun

You do not need to travel miles to be able to enjoy camping. Your backyard can be one cheaper and less-stressful place to have camping with your family or friends. Just make sure to make the ambience conducive to camping. If you want, you can even invite your nosy neighbours to join you.

Purchase annual passes – Low Cost Amusement

Amusement and water parks usually offer annual tickets that do not cost much. Take advantage of these offers if your family is into this type of entertainment.

Enjoy YouTube – Free Techie Fun

The Internet technology now offers free

entertainment via online videos. YouTube is the most popular source of these videos. You can also watch movies through other free movie sites.

Belt it out – Enjoy and Learn while Saving Money

If you do not have a karaoke microphone, you can borrow from your friends. There is also an online version of karaoke that you can also use as a form of free entertainment.

Play Online Games – Not Just for Kids but for Your Wallet's Health, too

There are millions of free online games that you can enjoy with your kids. Whether you want to play word games or puzzle games, the variety of online games is endless.

Set a Family Day – Regular Way to Save Money and Have Fun

Whether you play scrabble, go camping in your backyard, or watch online videos, setting a regular family day doing these simple and yet fun activities will condition your family to look forward to less-expensive ways of having fun. It is a great way to bond with your family members, as well.

Chapter 24: Benefits of a Recession

Would you believe that there are benefits to a recession? Yes there are and by knowing what they are, you can take advantage of them.

As a result of the recession, majority of the bonds and stocks are undervalued. This means you can buy these at reasonable prices. Just make sure you do some research first because you only want to buy those that have a good return when the economy recovers. You should also look into buying some property given that their value is also low.

Since you are a consumer, you will also get tax breaks. What happens here is that you don't have to pay that much income tax this year as a direct result of a deduction for private mortgage insurance which happens to be an extension of the sales tax write-off and also a boost in the alternative minimum tax exemption amount.

Aside from the Internal Revenue Service, the Federal Reserve also does its share to help the economy by slashing interest rates. This means you can borrow money at a lower rate as long as you have good credit ratings.

For those who are employed, a recession increases your retirement account limits. This can be done by using your rebate check to turbo charge your retirement savings and investing this in a Roth or

Traditional IRA. In the UK this will ISA, Pension etc. There are some people who have decided to invest it in both.

The environment also gets benefits from a recession. How? By making people make reductions in their expenses. For instance, car owners will trade their SUV's for smaller vehicles and people are less likely to travel for vacation. As a result, it will reduce the number of carbon gases that are released into the atmosphere.

This will also help boost online businesses since people will order items instead of driving over to the mall and make the roads less congested so there will be fewer traffic jams.

For those who want a career boost, this is the best time to go back to school since no one is hiring. Take a course that will enable you to switch to a better career or get an MBA. The current recession is not expected to go away this year so weigh your educational options.

Indeed, there are benefits to a recession but most of us don't see it because of how the media depicts it as a very bad thing. Now that you know that it is not entirely true, you just have to make the most of it until things do improve.

Chapter 25: Why you shouldn't worry about Economic Recessions

If there's one thing that can be said to symbolize today's society, it is the expectation of instant gratification. We want what we want, and we want it now. We have cars that drive over two hundred miles per hour, jets that break the sound barrier and rockets that go into outer space. We are constantly expanding our horizons, stretching our capabilities beyond the bounds of human comprehension, and pushing into unknown territory with each breath we take.

It's never occurred to us that we are not intended to do most of the things we do in the name of progress. If you had asked our ancestors two hundred years ago if we would ever go into space, they would have told you that if God had intended for us to fly he did have given us wings. Yet here we are. We have accomplished the impossible, and rather than being satisfied with that we push ourselves harder to accomplish the impossible faster and more spectacularly than ever before.

Fast food, microwaves, mail order videos and payday loans have encouraged us to think as far ahead as the next forty eight hours when it comes to our goals and expectations. We are lured, tempted and taunted by promises of overnight riches on the Internet with almost no work at all, and we have long since lost our appreciation for the toil and frustration of hard labour in favour of replaced those outdated methods of getting things done with updated technology that can accomplish the same thing in half the amount of time.

We live in a now society, which is why economic recessions are so difficult for us to accept. If we have a limited amount of capital coming and going, and a limited amount of growth happening in industries all across the world, we can't accomplish our goals in a short amount of time. We might even have to set those goals aside in favour of meeting our short term needs, such as keeping food on the table, or the long term, like building our retirement savings. Without booming enterprise we can't live the American dream and start our own business, because we need to provide our family with the security that the daily grind provides-and with millions of people across the country getting laid off every day, we're just happy to have a job.

What many people fail to understand is that economic recession is simply a normal part of the regular cycle of the business world. Although some recessions are more dramatic than others, the bottom line is that economic recessions happen regularly. If we didn't have economic recessions from time to time to the business world would be in trouble.

Economic recessions:
1. Cull out businesses that aren't going to survive the long haul. If you look at any guide to surviving an economic recession they will tell you that the most important thing to do is to either work for or run a company that is

going to continue to thrive even in the face of economic recession. Apple, IBM and Microsoft are not going anywhere, no matter how ugly the recession gets. Companies that provide basic needs like electric and food will always be in demand, because they have a product that is always going to have a need.

2. Wipe scams off the market. When economic recessions first begin they provide an atmosphere for get-rich-scams to thrive because people are desperate to break free of the sharp constrictions on their income that the recession and the accompanying consequences, as the recession drags on people are going to be too busy pumping their income into legitimate businesses trying to keep their heads above water to keep these frauds afloat. Sooner or later they are going to have to get a real job.

3. Force the government to tighten the strings on its budget. It's one thing to be able to spend exorbitantly when taxpayers can afford the inflation that goes along with it, but when taxpayers have to start counting their pennies the government has to tighten its belt right along with them and start funnelling the funds that it has coming in into productive programs that are going to do more than suck resources.

4. Drive down prices. Without economic recessions there would be nothing driving

down the price of goods and services, and our inflation would be even more ridiculous than it already is. When goods aren't selling, companies have to drive their prices down to make them more appealing or they will completely lose their investment-and they hate doing that.

Throughout history there have been many, many instances of economic recession. Think about the Great Depression back in the '30s. For two years in the early '80s there was a recession, and July 1990-March 1991 and November 2001-November 2002 were classified as economic recessions as well. Some of these periods inspired a tighter pinch on the pocketbooks of American citizens than others, but they happened.

After each of these recessions came periods of economic growth that allowed companies to get back on their feet and the economy to start flowing again as families had more money to spend. Economic recessions are nothing new. It's how we deal with them that determine the effect they are going to have on our economy.

Chapter 26: The Difference between letting yourself Thrive...

When people think about an economic recession the first thought that comes to mind is, "What am I going to do?" Their primary concern is for how they are going to be able to meet their financial obligations with the economy slipping steadily away.

That is a legitimate concern, and one that symbolizes a sense of responsibility. Unfortunately, there are some ugly side effects to economic recessions. Companies have to trim the fat in order to ride out the fact that consumers are plugging less and less money into their business, and usually that fat comes in the form of non-essential personnel. In other words, if you aren't on their list of most needed people your job will be the first to go when they are looking for a way to cut-back.

They can always replace you when things start picking back up. You wouldn't be human if you weren't a little concerned with how you are going to pay your bills in the face of an economic recession. The good news is that if you know the steps to take to protect your job and your company you can minimize the damage when it all hits the fan. As a matter of fact, with a little bit of effort and some savvy investing that would put the rookies on Wall Street to shame you can do much more than minimize the damage. You can make the recession work for you.

108

Chapter 27: Stock Market Investments

As businesses begin to lose money and booming, raging profits give way to something a little more on par with their daily expenses the door to successfully investing in the market swings wide open and invites you in. The principles of investing in the stock market during a recession are remarkably similar to the principles of investing in real estate. When you invest in the stock market during a recession you have the opportunity to take advantage of a company's poor fortune.

How? When companies are making money hand over fist the value of the company goes through the roof, and as the value of the company rises so too does the value of its stock. So when a company is riding high the price of the stock is going to be high as well. Shift the situation a bit, however, and the story changes.

Take mortgage giant Fannie Mae. In the month of July 2008 alone the value of its stock fell from $16 and change to a little over $8 a share. By September of that same year the share price was under a dollar courtesy of the sheer quantity of its borrowers that had defaulted on their loans.

Fannie Mae is only one of many companies who suffered a similar fate during the last recession. It is situations like these that present stock holders willing to think in the long term with a golden opportunity to make a profit. If they can purchase the shares when they are low, as in Fannie Mae's case, less than 1/16 their value, they can sit back, fold their hands and wait for the recession to end. When the recession has ended they can sell their shares for a tidy profit, sit back and pat themselves on the back for a job well done.

That doesn't mean you should go out, find a company that's failing and throw your life savings into their stock. That is a recipe for disaster that many investors have fallen into over the years!

This is a golden opportunity that definitely should not be allowed to pass you by, but there are a few things you should watch out for.

1) First and foremost, when you are choosing a company to invest in it is essential that you choose one that is going to weather the storm of the recession and bounce back when the time comes. If you sink your savings into a company and it goes under as a result of the recession you are going to be no better off than you were before. To determine whether or not a company will survive to see a bright new future rather than being pulled out when the recession separates the wheat from the chaff, answer the following questions:

    a. How long have they been in business? Companies that have been in business for many years are unlikely to go under because of a simple recession-in fact; they have likely weathered many of them in their time. A company that is already proven their staying power is an excellent choice of investment, and should definitely be given first consideration.

b. What do they do? Although companies that specialize tend to be movers and shakers when the economy is normal, if they are unable to expand and "macro" themselves (a topic we'll talk about in greater detail in just a bit) to adjust to the changing economy they are going to go under. If a company has not been able to expand and diversify, and if it doesn't offer a product that people are guaranteed to need day after day and therefore are pretty much guaranteed to keep coming back for, it is at a high risk for going under during the recession and should be given a wide berth.

c. Is their industry stable? Historically, there are certain industries that tend to fare better in a recession than others, and these should be given firm consideration when you are expanding your portfolio. Utility stocks (telephone, electric, gas), food and "escapes" such as cigarettes, alcohol and gambling have a history of tremendous success when it comes to riding out a recession because these are the industries that most consumers deem necessities and will continue pumping their money into.

d. Is it a necessity? The industries listed above are stable choices during a recession because they are deemed to be necessities; however, if there is one industry that you can be sure is not going to go anywhere in the face of any kind of recession, it is the healthcare and pharmaceutical industry. Regardless of what the economy looks like, people are going to get sick and they are going to need their medication to recover. This is a strong, stable choice for your portfolio, and it is one that you can count on to bring in a steady, if not always remarkable, return.

e. What about gold? Gold isn't going anywhere. If you are looking for a safe, solid and low risk investment during a recession period, gold is an excellent choice. There is very little chance that the value of gold is going to depreciate rapidly, and it's definitely not going anywhere.

f. Successful investing is not always just a matter of knowing what to invest in. Many times, it is also a matter of knowing what not to invest in. There are certain industries that often bring about good returns when the stock market is high, but who are extremely risky during times of recession. Can you guess which industries those are? Right. Any industry that specializes in luxury services is going to take a hit when conscientious investors start counting their pennies, and as a result so are their stockholders. Good industries to avoid include airlines, luxury resorts, restaurants (unless they have been around for a while) and, of course, financial and lending institutions (who are likely to go under as their borrowers slip further and further into debt).

g. If you are not familiar with the process of investing the best thing you could do for yourself to ensure the continued growth and success of your investments is find a skilled financial counsellor and/or investment broker to work with. Ideally, they will be able to look at a company's past history and their current place on the market and let you know whether or not they are a good choice for investment. Choose your broker with care, however; the last thing you want is to see your hard work and cautious planning fall apart because your broker was overly ambitious and pushed you into an investment that was doomed to failure from the very beginning.

2) Diversify. Regardless of how established a company is, there is no way to positively predict how they are going to react in the event of a recession. Your mother always told you not to put all of your eggs in a single basket, and she was absolutely right. If you can spread your investments around a bit through several companies in a variety of industries you will stand a better chance of being able to profit from this recession. Even if the bottom falls out of one and it goes under as a result of the poor economy you will have the others to fall back on and ensure that you are never left holding absolutely nothing at the end of the day.

Like real estate, investing in stocks now opens the door to the possibility of tremendous profits down the road. You may not be able to enjoy the same $100,000 gain you would have had you chosen to invest in houses rather than stocks, but you will enjoy a comfortable profit that will help carry you through on into the new economy.

Picture this. Let's say that you decided to take advantage of Fannie Mae's current position and bout 10,000 shares of stock. (For the record, this is not something I recommend; Fannie Mae is simply a hypothetical example for the purpose of this book). At today price of 49cent each, you did be able to acquire the stocks for under $4,900.

Not a bad day's work, all in all. You set the stocks aside and forget about them as the recession draws to a close. Somehow Fannie Mae has managed to weather the recession, and because of it your stocks rise in value back to their original price of $16 a piece. That means that the stocks you purchased during the recession, the ones that you paid 49cent for, are now worth thirty two times their original value. That means that instead of the $4,900 worth of stock you thought you had, you're now sitting on $160,000 worth of stock.

That is a $155,100 gain. $155.100, 2 year's worth of salary for part of America's citizens (4 years' worth for many) to get you started in your new life, all because you had the good sense to invest in the stock market when the selling price was low and the stocks were being agreeable. You saw the opportunity and you took it, and now you're going to reap the rewards.

Chapter 28: A Virtual Treasure Trove -the other Hidden Benefits of Recession

Economic recessions are a vital part of the economy, and they can play a huge role in helping you and your company look forward to a bright new future. These are not the only benefits of a recession though! Now that the heavy-duty stuff is out of the way, let's take a second look at some of the lighter benefits of a recession-the little day to day perks that will help you get through until the investment of your time and your money and your willingness to take the long term view pay off and you are able to enjoy everything that recession has to offer.

Riding in Style has Never Been So Easy

Earlier in this book I talked about how the real estate market responded to recession, and how the freefalling values of the housing market presented investors with real promise. The good news is that stocks and houses aren't the only things that tend to freefall in value when a recession happens!

If you have been holding out on buying that convertible or SUV of your dreams, now is the time to do it. Along with houses, cars are selling for pennies on the dollar what you would have paid for them before the recession. This is especially true of luxury vehicles, vehicles with poor gas mileage or other cars that simply are not considered to be high quality commuting vehicles. These vehicles are so unpopular that they are sitting around on lots right now gathering dust and waiting for someone to come take them home.

Someone like you, perhaps?

I will bet you never actually imagined that an economic recession could help you fulfil your dreams, did you? That is just another of the hidden benefits of recession that no one talks about because they are so busy hemming and hawing over the downsides. The simple fact of the matter is that an economic recession starts driving the prices back down of everything whose prices have been going up in the last few years in the face of an economic boom-and if you happened to take into consideration the fact that the price of gas is driving people to purchase small, functional commuting vehicles rather than luxury models or SUV gas guzzlers you find yourself with another golden opportunity staring you right in the face.

For example, a used car lot somewhere out west recently posted on its website the SUVs that had been sitting on their lots for an extended period of time. These SUVs had originally sold for $24,000 (ish). They were now on sale for under $15,000 and still gathering dust. You can only imagine what they will eventually sell for as the economy continues to fall. Imagine being able to purchase an SUV that once upon a time would have sunk you far into debt for less than 50% of their original value. How can you argue with that?

You can find anything Second-hand cheap when people are trying to save money rather than spend it they are also trying to earn it, which means that second-hand sales abound. (Coincidentally, an economic recession is also a great time to be a pawnbroker.) If you are looking for something, chances are good that somewhere out there someone is selling it. That encompasses everything from socks to hardware to little red wagons and back again. This is a prime time to take advantage of the number of second-hand opportunities that are going to be available and do some things that you've been putting off for a while now.

What can you find second-hand? Virtually everything. Somehow, no matter how odd an object is there is inevitably someone somewhere who considered it to be an equally good investment, and now with an economic recession staring them in the face the need to get rid of the objects in question is almost overwhelming. That means that regardless of what you are looking for, between the multitude of Goodwill, Salvation Army and consignment shops that about from coast to coast, it is bound to exist somewhere. The Bottom Line

The bottom line is that when it comes to surviving-no, thriving-in the midst of an economic recession, it all comes down to thinking in the long term. You are going to have to have the courage to take a chance where most people would tell you no chance should be taken and leave behind the expectations of instant gratification that plague so many people in today's society and instead grab on to the opportunities presented courtesy of the economic recession with both hands.

If you can have the courage to reach out and make those investments in the first place, and if you can have the patience and the perseverance to ride out the recession and eventually enjoy all of the benefits that the end of a recession inevitably brings, then you have what it takes to overcome the recession and survive, thrive and walk away with your pride, your bank account and your retirement fund firmly intact.

Chapter 29: Conclusion

There are many ways to use an economic recession to improve your future and reap a profit; however, most of these methods require you to take a long term view on the effects of the recession, and to sit back and allow the poor economy to roll right over you. That is a great attitude to take if you have hundreds of thousands of dollars sitting in the bank and can afford to wait the economy out; however, if you are like most of the rest of us you are operating on a tight budget even when the economy is booming!

If you are barely getting by when the economy is good, how on earth are you going to manage to keep your head above water when recession is flooding businesses from coast to coast? It can be done, if you're smart enough and savvy enough to look for the hidden opportunities hiding behind every misfortune.

There is no doubt about it, the economic recession that's raging across the world courtesy of an absurd number of layoffs, massive quantities of homeowners defaulting on their mortgages, an inflation rate that far overpowers current adjustments to incomes and the resulting decrease in consumer spending has hit everyone hard. As Americans struggle to pay their bills and put enough away to ensure their retirement, companies from coast to coast are taking a major hit in profits.

Somehow purchasing a new Ferrari just doesn't look as appealing when you consider the impact that expense is going to have on your retirement account.

The bad news is that this trend doesn't show any immediate signs of coming to an end, particularly as gas prices continue to soar. The good news is that an economic recession is not always a bad thing! In fact, if you are a savvy investor and business owner an economic recession can actually help you. Why? Because there are certain things that happen during a recession that, if used correctly, can help you ensure your security and the security of your family for many years to come.

It seems as though every time you turn on the news there is another story about a plant that is closing, another company that is outsourcing their labour and laying off their employees and a rapidly growing line of people standing in the unemployment office. What they don't tell you about are the hundreds of people behind the scenes who are benefitting from this economic recession. Why should they? Good news doesn't make good news!

I firmly believe if we are going to have our lives and our futures tossed like a boat in a storm courtesy of an economic recession, every man, woman and child has the right to know how to secure that future through the opportunities that are staring them right in the face. That is what this book is all about! As individuals we can't change a single thing that is going on "out there". What we can do is change the way we look at it and learn to seek out the hidden jewels of opportunity that make economic recessions a gold mine for the savvy investor.

www.ingramcontent.com/pod-product-compliance
Lightning Source LLC
Chambersburg PA
CBHW051719170526
45167CB00002B/719